BLANK BOOK OF SHADOWS
YOUR PERSONAL BOOK OF SPELLS

www.ingramcontent.com/pod-product-compliance
Lightning Source LLC
LaVergne TN
LVHW082300150826
845677LV00009B/1678

* 9 7 9 8 8 6 9 4 5 8 6 3 6 *